HOUSES

ALSO BY DON BARKIN

The Caretakers (chapbook)

That Dark Lake

The Persistent (chapbook)

HOUSES

New and Selected Poems

by Don Barkin

Antrim House
Simsbury, Connecticut

Copyright © 2017 by Don Barkin

Except for short selections reprinted for purposes of
book review, all reproduction rights are reserved.
Requests for permission to replicate should
be addressed to the publisher.

Library of Congress Control Number: 2016962806

ISBN: 978-1-943826-22-3

First Edition, 2017

Printed & bound by Ingram Spark, LLC

Book design by Rennie McQuilkin

Front cover painting by Peter Van Dyck

Author photograph by Maggie Barkin

Antrim House
860.217.0023
AntrimHouse@comcast.net
www.AntrimHouseBooks.com
21 Goodrich Road, Simsbury, CT 06070

For Steve Barkin, logician

Thanks to the editors of the following publications, in which poems from this collection first appeared, sometimes in earlier versions:

Confrontation: "War Poem"

Commonweal: "Houses," "The 'Strengthless Arms of the Baggage Handlers," "Erratum to an Elegy for a Doomed Youth," "In Sun and Shade," and "Genius is Cheapness"

The Cortland Review: "The Persistent," "Ode to Rte. 6 West-bound"

The Florida Review: "A Ghost"

Freshwater: "An Old Maker," "Awakening," "Nieces on the Beach"

Harvard Magazine: "Rain," "Wedding Poem"

Interim: "A Quiet Incident," "The Swimmers"

The Louisville Review: "Last Words," "Sliding"

Mudfish: "After Armstrong," "Snapshot of a Chinese Baby"

The New Formalist: "Lost in the Woods," "The Sun"

North American Review: "Brown Bouquets"

Poetry: "The Caretakers"

Poetry Northwest: "The Room"

Prairie Schooner: "Fast Food," "The Two"

Press: "In the Kitchen," "School Photographer"

The Raintown Review: "At the Edge"

Verse: "End Song"

The Virginia Quarterly Review: "Grief," "Informal Logic," "The Mathew Brady Photographs"

Some of these poems appeared in different forms in a previous book, *That Dark Lake* (Antrim House Books, Simsbury, Connecticut, 2009) and in an earlier chapbook, *The Caretakers* (Finishing Line Press, Georgetown, Kentucky, 2008).

The author would like to thank the State of Connecticut for two Individual Artist Grants.

TABLE OF CONTENTS

I.

Genius is Cheapness / 4
Houses / 5
In Sun and Shade / 6
Marginalia / 7
The Blimp / 8
Walking Clouds the Mind / 9
Erratum to an Elegy for a Doomed Youth / 10
The "Strengthless Arms" of the Baggage Handlers / 11
He Plays No Favorites / 12
In the Medical Building / 13
The Persistent / 14
The Ruins of the First Private Pool in This City / 15
Dispatch from Ft. Lewis / 16
The Words of Our World / 17
Visiting the Tomb / 18
The Historic House on the Hill / 19
The Park Committee's Placards / 20
A Walk and Then a Drive / 21
Men Spend Their Days Indoors Like Fish / 22
The Docent in his Dotage / 23
Chewed-Off Wing on the Lawn / 24
Four Seasons / 25
La Résistance des Animaux / 26
Time Of Course / 27
Sunny and Warmer / 28
The Only Honor / 29

Cut Down / 30
Fly on the Window / 31
Ode to Ambition / 32
At the Lake / 33
Sunday Evening / 34

II.

On the Thruway / 36
Ode to Rte. 6 / 37
The Frozen Falls Behind the Library / 38
A Hungry Generation / 39
An Old Maker / 40
Boy in August / 41
Brown Bouquets / 42
To a Teacher / 43
Lost in Woods / 44
A Peaceful Cemetery / 45
At the Edge / 46
A Graveyard Tale / 47
The Smell We Tracked Down / 48
A Reunion / 49
The Life / 50
Back Out / 51
Road Rage / 52
Evening Walk / 53
A Ghost / 54
In Middle Age / 55
Home Improvement / 56

A Snow Bank in April / 57

An Accident in Space / 58

Three Straight Days of Rain / 59

An Information Age / 60

The Ice Storm / 61

School Photographer / 62

A Religious Illusion / 63

To a Graduate / 64

The Nature Lover / 65

The Moon and Me / 66

On a Daughter Gone Abroad / 67

A Brief Freedom in Youth / 68

Comrades / 69

Two on Marriage / 70

Stuck in Snow / 71

Nieces on the Beach / 72

Why She Went / 73

Schooled / 74

Why Old Men Should be Sad / 75

About the Author / 76

HOUSES

I.

Genius is Cheapness

Or call it a craftsman's thriftiness.
The skinflint Ford, wincing at
a workman hunting for his hammer,
said a man is a hammer and his friend a wrench.
Edison, liking the ring
of *Let there be,* tried this, then that
for a filament that would sing like the sun.
Einstein also, the sockless one,
did what does not require socks.

The gold-nibbed physician Sigismund,
impatient with the rictus of women,
thought all of it was this – just *this*.
And Henry David, the handyman,
shook life like a Christmas tree
until it breathed free of its tinsel
and sprang up like a brickyard weed –
and God and everybody laughed
at how few moves to make all this.

Houses

Given gravity, it is only right
that the houses hunched along the road
seem substantive and unconcerned.
Yet their great weight distorts the air,
as the castle in the fish's bowl
makes the fish seem ill at ease,
unsuited to its situation.

The soul if it is a point,
a tiny point adrift within,
can not answer their harrumph
nor penetrate their shingled bulk
to coats hung in their mudrooms.
The passing man is himself a bowl,
and his soul a fish that hovers there.

He feels it drifting through his skull,
a blinking thing with things to say
if only it could find its tongue,
as sunrooms drawl of ottomans
and concrete steps with wrought-iron rails
say all there is to say about
coming in and going out.

In darkened dens, glowing bowls
sit silently on polished tops
while ashy flakes come drifting down.
So the soul is fed on flakes of wonder –
the passing man senses it
rise open-mouthed and then dart down
to storm around its quavering castle.

In Sun and Shade

In a small town, people are
who they are, no getting away
from what the eighth-grade teacher thinks,
the ex-wife, the hardware guy.
And when the sun at 3 o'clock
passing through this civic prism
dyes the flaking stucco wall
of Magruder's Service Station, the side
by the vacant lot where sharp things rust,
that is where the spirits mingle,
the ones you know or who know you.
And if on foot you stop to gawk
why, there you are among the shades.
Still the wall can't tell you what you feel
about who you are or wish to be –
the life you've led, the love you've won.
And who knows what Magruder feels,
who sometimes pays to have it painted
and has himself a wild tattoo
on his upper arm, his wife Leona's
name in flames, for what that's worth?

Marginalia

Real order is the milk of one mind –
not the conference but the bored professor
who drifting out to the gaudy lobby
sniffs like Schliemann the sadness of Troy
in the laminate and the tinny tunes.

Then why a *rubric*? Why a *benchmark*?
And why a calendar like a branding iron
burning into our breathing flank,
and staking out the meadow that
stretched fenceless to a foggy copse?

Let doodles be dashed off then
or cross-hatched with mammal fury
and neither bad nor good, but like our lives –
a heavy-leaded nose in profile
sniffing at a glum agenda.

The Blimp

Silent as the shadow of a cloud
you startle two men fishing from a boat
who, feeling a sullen chill, look up
at that distinguished thing, a drifting hill.
While what you see from your ungoverned height
is things are roughly what you always thought,
though stiller and untroubled by their state.

That chapter over, you go sweetly on
still swimming with the wind, and on a whim
lift free from all that's local and complete,
though no less curious about what lies
beyond that bank of woods, the curving earth.
With your green gases softly seeping out,
you're free to travel where your lack of plans

won't let you down, fields no one owns,
where, eager as a child who jogs ahead
of heavy-legged grownups toward the tent,
everything is something you once dreamt:
a pleasant-looking lady strokes her beard,
a fat man lounges on his throne of fat,
and someone's drunken uncle guzzles fire.

Walking Clouds the Mind

Who said this rock here, that broken branch
there along somebody's lawn?
And there, who said those flakes of paint
shaken from a rotten sash
dragged on concrete to a truck
to crown a midden at the dump?
What star-stained hand yanked on a shaft
now to make snowflakes fall
like blossoms on the lawn, and now
to pound the shell-pocked town with shells?

We know we'll never catch Him up
who waits like grass somewhere for us.
Instead: that dent in the dusty truck
bucking past to fix a leak –
the plumber can't recall the ding
among such things that have happened to him
in torn-off months like the bleached receipts
between the dash and dusty glass,
while empty coffees roll around
like planets on the oily mat.

Erratum to an Elegy for a Doomed Youth

Sometimes you just don't know –
you just don't know how things,
you just don't know how things will turn out.

You knew – or you thought you knew.
You could see the way the road
was going – there, and over the rise.

It's not that you were wrong
or right. You never knew, but what
you felt, or feared, and could taste.

Then when cresting the slow rise --
not a valley of alfalfa and the yellow wheat
but a buzzing district of current and errands.

Not as beautiful as the wheat,
but the needful – the vague mountains
tethered to the cement town.

This is where you've never been.
Though slowly you start to realize
that God must surprise Himself, or no dice.

The "Strengthless Arms" of the Baggage Handlers

Athough you have never seen them yourself,
there are places you still suppose to exist.
San Diego, for example,
where the man in the next cubicle
flew his family over Christmas week . . .
Beautiful weather, a wonderful zoo!
You imagine a sun-splashed elephant
in its glaring enclosure – San Diego.

Not for the Louvre you flew to Paris,
but the baggage handlers who came at dawn
on a grimy tram to stack big bags
in the shadow of the Eiffel Tower
yet would not lift their eyes to it.
Now if you wondered what difference
anything makes, you could go home
and live as a man who has been to France.

Another place you suppose to exist
entered your mind one afternoon
asleep underneath the Sunday papers.
In the Travel Section, in gaudy orange,
was an ancient desert habitation
and a man on his camel. Like you on your couch,
he too will go, when his god wills it so,
to a place even stranger than San Diego.

He Plays No Favorites

Although we know that some of us won't make it
we also know He never meant anything by it.
And this is roughly what we mean by Heaven.
Plus "luck" is not a word in his High Hebrew.
To stretch a point, He'll daub a grateful grin
on a bald child and those who change her sheets.
Still we feel the suns as cold that come without them,
and hate the pain that hounded them to their graves.
What must console us – He never meant anything by it.

In the Medical Building

In the end he just clomped down
flights of fire-stairs
like pounding down a trail
in the shade of trees.
The thudding of his boots
was his heart out of his chest.

Never again the theatrical
sigh of the elevator
with its misted silver doors
parting in the middle
on a glossy bronze plaque
and a feathered arrow west.

Just his clumsy thud
on the cloudy gray concrete.
Then through the mirrored lobby
like a man passing through Heaven
to scrape ice-cream from a cup
and walk with her survivors.

The Persistent

He swims every day all year,
wading in from any beach
wherever he happens to be –
glistening resort or grimy port-town –
remembering the heft of the tide
and where the bottom dropped off.
His plunging hardly leaves a ripple.
The water wants to bear him up
and he passes through it graciously
as a congressman or a widow.
You lose him for a frightening while.
Until he appears clambering
onto a rock you hadn't noticed
sticking up, so far away
he seems almost to be standing on air.

The Ruins of the First Private Pool in This City

At one end deep as bulkhead steps,
its bottom batched with Roman scraps,
this ruined pool recalls those gods
who fluttered down like furling leaves
when Heaven's winds were shuttered up.
Here once a wife concealed her curls
beneath a creamy rubber cap
and slipped from shadow into shadow
elusive as a swift or nymph
where shaggy oaks waved strangers off.

Though now a silver chain-link fence
makes the place a horrid hole,
this opulence in cement
which once contained a bright content
still wills suave gods of banking back.
To you, the grimy white walls say,
"Nothing noble ever goes
astray from such a shapen place,
and we only see how dangerous
the deep-end was in vivid air."

Dispatch from Ft. Lewis

We are still out here, Sir, fighting the Indians.
It's funny how these yellow plains
look empty enough until like a cloud
you'd swear wasn't there a minute ago,
a slew of them howl down on us.
Or you thought you heard birds screaming
a mile off, but it wasn't birds.
I know (I was raised up in the church)
it's not right to fight these savages –
instead we should help them with their lot.
But just the thought of schools set up
and men in collars telling them
to sell their pots and figuring
the price of the pots and loading them up –
it heavies my heart. Let me draw a bead
and pick one off his Palamino,
so riding dead against its neck
like taking a nap, that bastard tumbles
in the long grass. Their fast ponies
obey them like their quiet women.
Sometimes you get one in the blue
gaze of your Winchester
and wince to even squeeze the trigger.
Hell, what's the use of men like me?
We don't grow wheat, we don't raise up
the steeple of a new church.
Our wives, if we've got them, wince when we speak.
But what can you do, Sir, if you are a varmint?
Respectfully, Smith – Yr. Man Out Here.

The Words of Our World

Credit card is the ugliest sound
in the English tongue. And *cash*
doesn't sound much better although
softer in the mouth. *Broke*
is bad too, as cruel as the crush
of a shut front door. Or as *debt*
which stuffs its shirt with that *b*
which is better than *broke* or worse.

Well-off and *well-set* are also disgusting,
disguising theft with the word for *health*,
which must also be bought. And *greed* itself,
with its cache of vowels. Plus *generous*,
which arrives on a waft of minty breath,
suggesting a man with more than his share,
happy to help some wretch whose lips
puff out from a fist in the gut: *obliged!*

You could find all this in a dictionary,
but you'd miss the essential whiff of things –
the *whiz* of a thousand arrows aloft
above what was a farmer's field,
meaning *duck, bad luck,* and *history.*
Or, better, the *dog shit* on your shoe,
which followed you in from your evening walk
after work in this pleasant part of town.

Visiting the Tomb

When you descend into a tomb
it isn't the tincture of death you sniff
but the musk of Time. The misty mind
cools to dew where mushrooms glow.
So the man goes home, a citizen
of the empire of things that simply exist,
shining like dust in the darkened parlor.

Take Abraham Lincoln in his tomb
where it may be there molders still
a shred of frock, of silky sock,
or even a shard of spindly digit.
You think you sniff him lifting off
to History. But he's heading for
the bleachers, where he'll lose that hat.

The Historic House on the Hill

A fresh coat of paint is a statement of sorts.
If the paint is white, it is a statement of faith.
But what faith? The prig who built this
looked to the Lord. But it was the impulse
that mattered most. When he looked up
from his farmer's field, the snath of his scythe
slick with sweat, the house on the hill
dazzled his mind like a white flame –
light sent with a will from Heaven
and welcomed with a coat of white paint,

And so, although the joists groaned
and rats ran in the attic and the cellar,
when spring came he scraped and repainted.
Which is why we preserve the white house
which was never a church, but an urgency.
It winks from its hill wordlessly
through this gloomy wilderness of words.
God hurls down His will in waves
and we gather it on our pale backs
and warmed to order, hack at the earth.

The Park Committee's Placards

As for littering, it is not open
to discussion. But consider the snug
nests of empties in their sacks,
the savaged wrappers of cigars,
condoms, and candy cast away
at the moment of someone's coming undone.

When the lady passed us on the path,
we greeted her with a bird's song –
with the bright trills of nervous birds
we greeted each other. All day our songs
went round in rounds, while men slept in
in rented rooms and woke to thunder.

A Walk and Then a Drive

As it happened, he drove along the road
he'd walked that morning, which went quickly past
in flashes of woods and brooks, and pebble pop,
reminding him of the difference between time,
which doesn't exist, and distance which does, but dully.

In the morning when he walked, the road
was lit with glints of wit and pools of gloom.
Those things belonged to time and so survived
only brokenly, as dreams survive to stain
our day, that are the purest proof of mind.

Men Spend Their Days Indoors like Fish

Depressives love the colors of
the linoleum – bad hamburger,
the blue of a harbor by Monet,
and halvah. Nor do the windows here

admit wind. The building is abuzz,
being regional and detail-driven.
The flagpole out front is at half-mast
for the soldiers and such. Its rigging chinks.

It is a building, and it has its reasons.
Though soon swung balls will bring it down.
On a far-off hard-drive a parking garage
slouches this way. Its flagpole will clang.

The Docent in His Dotage

When he'd named the *moose* he moved on,
having done the best that he could do,
then flowers and pests. Now it was his garden.

Lately, a lanky carpenter named *Will*
smiled lankily and muttered *Mark*. In time,
only *shit* and *piss* will hiss their names.

His wrinkled friends all hail him by name,
reminding him he never loved them much.
Boo, who bore his kids, still calls him *Bub*.

Chewed-off Wing on the Lawn

Like that Greek who set out again
in a ship fitted out with dead friends
who will never dispute what he says
but make him a hero again,
so the geezer uncorks his boast –
how one summer in his youth
he leaped like a wheel of fire
from a dangerous quarry face.

So what if the waitress, Jen,
him being over the hill,
will never console him in bed.
The ship that he shoves out
will still reach the Western Isles,
the sun sobbing in its sails.
For all hankering is as heroic
as a brown abandoned wing.

The Four Seasons

Fall, shawl, pall, bawl.
Winter, glinter, stinter, hinter.
Spring, wing, fling, ring.
Summer, slummer, strummer, dumber.

La Résistance des Animaux

When German jeeps patrolled the streets of Paris
and *une petite fille* displayed a weeping cheek,
they smacked it with a riding crop. So loping
along a country road beneath the trees,
you spot a crumpled can or a filthy
whiskey flask, and know an animal
will hurl itself beneath the whizzing tires
of a Jeep and make some blameless driver blanche.
Did you doubt this is a big business machine?
Nothing escapes its sprockets' perfect teeth.

Time of Course

Time of course flies forward
like an arrow. Though
sometimes it stands still.
Until we see
it is us standing still
and must hustle to reclaim
our place in Creation.

One thing we know: time
doesn't run backwards.
It just sticks out its tongue
in the rearview mirror
then runs in a house
while we take our wide turn
toward tomorrow.

Sunny and Warmer

This is the spirit of the neighborhood –
houses like battleships at anchor
and our dark angels of stone and gravel,
Miguel and Jesus, laying pavers.

While someone's mother watches TV
behind closed curtains – the news and weather –
and someone's son punishes his drums
in the muddy light of a rumpus room.

These are a sort of commentary –
more electric than the news and weather.
Plus the glum thrumming of buses and trucks.
And this is the spirit of the era.

The Only Honor

The only honor is to exist.
Not to be alive but exist
like everything . . . the trees, the sky.
This is why we do our best,
to drive a nail in straight,
to hold our heads up as the trees
seem to do. The sea to gleam.

This is the ghost that waves us away
from the lesser prizes – cash, acclaim,
those dust cloths on the furniture
of the great house in which we live.
Yet there is no one to thank or bow down to.
Just fill your lungs and let it out.
Wash your socks, then hang them up.

Cut Down

Not a sapling perhaps,
but a young or teenage tree
no fatter than your fist,

recently cut down
with a hacksaw like a harp
by one who knew his stuff.

Its face is wreathed with frowns
like a pebble in a pool
to prove it once drew breath.

Bad luck to have grown up
on a grassy sidewalk strip
and be sensibly edited out.

In woods it would have looked
up to a big oak
and mingled with its limbs

in the flapping tapestry
of the wilderness untouched
by human husbandry.

Look, a glove a gardener dropped.
So filthy and stiff, and yet
a hand once lived in it.

Fly at my Window

It's looking out, of course.
Funny they stand at the glass
which makes them easy to see
and whack them into goo.
They stand against the light
despite the pane of glass,
since light is what they love –
and the air the light lives in,
and the wind that tugs the air
as a lover tugs the sheet.
All of life, in short,
except the part indoors
where buzzing to and fro
they batten on the glass
and gaze at what seems close,
if only for the glass.

Ode to Ambition

Ambition, you cocksucker,
how many men have you wrecked
wearing out their delicate nibs
with the furious weight
of your wish to write in stone
your passing remarks on the frail paper
of their lives, fluttering leaves
that will never decorate a tree again.
Still you lean with your grunting weight,
desperate to rut into being
a line of kings stretching out
to the crack of doom.

At the Lake

Here light once landed *like*
a fly on a stallion's back,
a flapping honking flock,
the first word God spoke.
Then lengthened *like spilled milk,*
like a lover on her back.

Now it's a ski-loud lake,
words crumble like stale cake.
To a mind that's walked the plank
itself is what it's like.
And the sky above it blank,
and beneath that sky, your bank.

Sunday Evening

Pry his hands away from his plough,
and after two days he'll wander off
and drown in the thin froth of the stars.

It's Sunday dusk that is holy to him.
With his weak back and his dread of the weather,
still he champs to have at the Devil again.

And where else but the week to do the work
God hung him with – the mucky row,
as deaf to the distant hiss of the stars

as a pitcher to the howling crowd
who mops his brow to do for a buck
what he did in his father's yard for fun.

II.

On the Thruway

Struggling up the long hill,
you spot them at the crest.
They left us once and now they will
rejoin us without rest.

Surely this is Kingdom Come
where we were always going,
even if these dead are dumb
or can't admit to knowing.

But where you'd hit the shining skies
the future flattens out –
and then your look of wild surmise
resumes its thruway pout.

You feel like a child and sigh,
embarrassed to pretend
that dead men stand against the sky
then silently descend.

Ode to Rte. 6

The roadside grasses quiver in
a wave of air where cars have been
like knots of comets howling by,
too loud to hear the grasses sigh
as sleepers sigh when nightmares shake
them cruelly up but not awake.
The cars themselves are in a spell
and travel back and forth pell-mell,
trumpeting a new age
of information, speed, and rage.
Such sleek machines are bound to bring
a springtime sweeter than the spring.
The grass blades bending in a gust
all-hail them on their way to rust –
and then again the road is still,
with just a whiff of oil and will.

The Frozen Falls Behind the Library

Old age is a halted waterfall,
a charge the village honors with a wall
of glassy-eyed, ropey-throated vets.

But underneath the ice, grim rivulets
go groping on to launch their last attack
on God's guffawing guns, and not come back.

A Hungry Generation

Some kids fell in behind me. I liked their talk
which was mild and slow. Country kids I guessed
must watch less television. Still, when I walk
on country roads I like my own talk best.

Thoreau went to the woods to think things through
away from honest village voices. A brook
carried off the froth of what men knew.
Glimmering at its bottom was his book.

Their buzzing hung around me like a fly
the whole way back to town and our one store,
where louder now they crowded in to buy
the chips and soda they'd gone miles for –

then slid away like the stream Thoreau
called Time. "Poor kids," I thought, and let them go.

An Old Maker

The Miller Building hasn't been
occupied for years, although
the sun still loves it and looks in
through frosted panes that daze the flow
of light like sunshine ghosting through
a cloud of leaves to haunt your shoe.

Someone (we don't know his name)
once daubed a deer hunt on the face
of a cave lit only by a flame
to drive the darkness from that place.
Now cool as glass, he's traveled far
beyond his burning like a star.

Boy in August

He didn't seem to see me pass
standing dumbstruck in the grass
– a small boy staring past his feet
at his shadow in the heat.
It must have made him feel queer
the way the shadow didn't care
if no one called it to come in
or came to ask where it had been.
I thought, *Someday he'll like to go
to lakes where tall pine trees grow,
where the water is always darkly lit
and Heaven a dull gleam in it.*

Brown Bouquets

Pulling out of school, I saw the slew
of brown bouquets, brittle-looking flowers
beside the cross with not one name, but two,
dead boys. They'd been left out in sun and showers
as if to show you grief grown old in you.

I'd only seen the dead without their powers,
but fumbling for my seatbelt now I knew
that somehow I'd been in my final hours
when flowers told me what I had to do.
And boys give up their brittle lives for ours.

To a Teacher

First, do no harm, they warn all new physicians.
But it's harder than they think,
and discovering they're death as diagnosticians,
some linger at the sink.

Teachers too. For though she's seventeen,
that girl still chews her hair,
and while she turned her nose up like a queen,
your scolding drew a tear.

Still, teaching texts are careful not to use
the word that like a charm
(not "skill" or "grip" or "a talent to amuse")
can steer you clear of harm,

whatever clever lesson plans you make
based on the latest laws
of pedagogy. It's "love" for Heaven's sake
that gives your whip-hand pause.

Lost in Woods

The footprints in the snow were mine. "Oh, shit,"
which was a word I hardly ever said,
and there was no one else to laugh at it.
Sunset. By morning I'd be numb or dead.

Dusk in woods comes as a thickening
of a thousand things to one, as groping through
a darkened room where every homey thing
has forgotten itself, the room forgets you too.

I walked out on a road they hadn't plowed.
A man stood on his porch beneath the light
and smoked and heaved the smoke out in a cloud.
Then he went in and shut his front door tight.

A room turned blue behind its scrim of frost –
whatever else he was, he wasn't lost.

A Peaceful Cemetery

She took her final illness in her stride,
her obit crowed. He researched heart disease
and spoke at meetings right until he died –
not just in the States but overseas.

They once wore faces puckered with concern
about so many things, and then just one.
Past that now, they seem content to turn
their pale, pitted faces to the sun.

And losers, too. He stank and lived alone,
and something from the past amazed his face.
Yet every day he got up with a groan
and struck out like a pilgrim for this place.

But that boy drove here fast, too young to think
of waiting for disease or age or drink.

At the Edge

You can't take your eyes off the boy slumping
in the monstrous chair being wheeled
backwards into the college gym –
the way you stood in that roped-in field
gaping at the canyon's rim
and imagining yourself jumping.

A Graveyard Tale

"Father," "Mother," "Susan" – three
bleached headstones in a row,
but by her side where there should be
a husband, wildflowers grow.

She'd feared that as their child she
would be the last to go
and sleep beneath a stone marked "Me."
A fever took her though.

The Smell We Tracked Down

Sometimes things just don't smell right.
That rabbit by the water heater
lay dead in the dappled basement light
where no one's golden lab would eat her.

"Average folk can't live here now,"
our librarian said. She'd sold her place
to the Christian camp, and her furrowed brow
reminded me of the furious face

of that girl who worked at her father's store
downtown, was a whale, and never wed –
and that sullen stain on the basement floor.
The fox blames the trap, not itself, Blake said.

A Reunion

Spotting her first he knew he mustn't smile,
so if she suddenly turned and met his look
from halfway down the empty pet-food aisle,
she wouldn't sniff, *A fan of my new book*.

Though later lying sleeplessly in bed
he saw her face again – so paper blank
he'd dropped some dog food in his cart and fled,
thinking how she'd risen while he sank

to where he often came across her name
in magazines, while he still lay suspended
between the sunny ocean swell of fame
and its unlit floor. But if he felt upended,

he knew that in their dreaming time of life
they'd slumbered side by side like man and wife.

The Life

He'd stop the clock when she came in the room –
her grin that flicked the switch of every lamp
and poked the fire driving out the damp
and made the faded wall-paper flowers bloom

and made him feel a keenness in his heart
and think he must be handsome after all.
His trick of stopping time was just to stall –
before their talk of kids and chores could start

he'd turn back to his book and frown or sigh
so all the light bulbs flickered and the room
was cast half-back into the gloom
her coming had dispelled. While she stood by,

he'd grunt and jab the hearth until a spark
reared up to make her smile in the dark.

Back Out

That low impassioned drone
was no one on his phone
but a drunk my bike-lamp showed
lurching down the road

and pawing at the air
like a bee-crowned bear.
Yet as I cycled by
something in his eye

made a thudding start
in my rusted heart,
and I slowed my peddling
so I could hear him sing

the saga of a bum
which if its mood was glum
and its style uncouth,
rang like brass or truth.

Not that I would like
to get down off my bike
and hear a drunk confess –
and he would like it less.

Road Rage

She'd flung her cigarette
out the window as she tore
past me in her car
with her pedal to the floor,

where it glowed an instant more
although the road was wet
like a fallen star
that hasn't burned up yet.

I guessed a broken heart,
and though she made no sign
her fury made me feel
the fault must be mine.

Hearts that I once broke
shone coldly overhead.
Their light had just arrived
from stars I'd thought long dead.

And now I had to ask
if from across the years
someone had hurled her claim
for loving in arrears.

Evening Walk

I knew the house but not the man
sobbing by his garbage can.
He'd gone inside, undone his tie,
then come back out alone to cry.

His wife was dying in their bed.
Or his wife had packed a bag and fled.
I knew I'd been allowed to see
catastrophe catch up with me,

and would have hovered out of view
the way I skulk in graveyards too,
to hide myself from Heaven's spears
among men emptied of their tears.

A Ghost

A once-plush towel
with a worn-out look
hung from a hook
in the downstairs toilet
where little hands spoiled it
washing up in a hurry.
Behind it, its shadow
looked out like an owl
in a black, tangled tree
blanketed with snow.

Though small hands have fled
with the echo of their shout
the shadow still looks out
but at you instead
with an owl's glare.
It looks out to say
that someone was here
for a while and went away
as snow will disappear
that fell all day.

In Middle Age

In middle age you smell the end
the way you smell the snow
a frigid windless sky will send
when the sun is low.

Nonetheless you rise and think
about the day ahead,
and sip your coffee at the sink
and tug a little thread.

And while you buzz inside your hive
all day at work you know
(perhaps you fail, perhaps you thrive),
the sky is full of snow.

Home Improvement

"I g-guess I'd run a length of p-pipe downhill.
You don't w-want water rotting out your sill."
Not much gets past the censor of John's stutter
unless a buddy's got a puddling gutter.

"If we were tools," I mused, "what would we be?"
My wife had brought some beers to him and me.
"Like, you're a level." I meant his steady eye
that kept his cellar and his humor dry.

"And my wife's a trowel covering up mistakes
her hopelessly unhandy husband makes."
Well, I was never sent to Boy Scout camp
or watched my dad rewire a broken lamp.

Expect poison from standing water, warned Blake.
I went to get a shovel and a rake.

A Snow Bank in April

These random Alps of frozen snow
that though its April stop your feet
and make you lift your head and go
dazed into the empty street

are monuments to a storm
that may have raged two days and nights,
and even now the days are warm
glimmer like glum Christmas lights.

The snow, though gray-faced with exhaust,
is frozen hard as any heart
that clenched against an early frost
and threatens blossoms when they start.

But blossoms always have their day
then yield to leaves which reign a season,
wither, fall, and fly away,
then drifts that halt the feet and reason.

An Accident in Space

On any other day you would have seen
– well, if you'd happened to look – the silver wink
of business class from Dallas. A bird would mean
whatever a bird alone in the sky made you think.

I squinted at the sun but couldn't tell.
They weren't shooting stars since it was day,
but something pod-like burst and its seeds fell
like fire through the blue and died away.

Meanwhile at his glowing screen or scope
somebody with earphones on his head
must have once imagined he heard hope.
It twittered like a swallow then went dead.

The glittering stars that night looked like the spray
of windshield glass they never sweep away.

Three Straight Days of Rain

I thought He'd left us all for dead
the way He did in Noah's day
when clouds rolled in at dawn to stay,
then rain to make us snug in bed.

Though now the clouds have exited
and left me blameless under blue,
I'd rather know what Noah knew
about our cloudy sense of dread.

As I know clomping gloomily
down the cellar stairs sometimes
in dungeon darkness that my crimes
have finally caught up with me.

As having shook the attic beams
with my heavy gallows tread
on the staircase up to bed,
He's laying for me in my dreams.

An Information Age

Freeze or flee a hulking bear?
And jumper-cables – which goes where?
I've cocked my head at those who knew
and blinked as soon as they were through.

I guess my tribe was left behind
when Adam, bored of being blind,
converted men to cleverness –
from playing house to playing chess,

who peck at data like a chicken
and snack on news until they sicken,
judging any man a wuss
who'd bend to fate like Oedipus.

Still some men will not take the bait
of trying to outfox their fate
like that great king who wept because
he'd never quite known who he was.

The Ice Storm

A freezing rain has glazed the snow
and littered it with shards of trees.
The limbs that haven't snapped hang low,
barely lifting in the breeze.
Our neighbor and his nine-year-old
go by in boots and neither speaks.
The sun must have gotten cold
to paint that orange on their cheeks

Sitting in this living room
with music and a good fire,
the whispering of my wife's broom
on the kitchen floor, the thumping dryer
in the cellar, and our daughter dressing dolls,
I watch the flames until I see
the windows darken a degree,
and icicles run down these walls.

School Photographer

It's the boys who look like they might cry.
So, I spin around and scuttle back,
head down, to my black-
cloaked camera to grin once more
at a beefy boy with a fat tie,
raked hair and frown, and roar,
"Sit up, son, good, now
look up at me, more to your right,
perfect, now say 'Gouda cheese.'
Okay, again!" Somehow
in my quick squinting sight
a blonde forelock becomes a bough
of forsythia bounced in a breeze
and a school-glazed eye as bright
as lakewater.
                We all come
from somewhere flaming, and whatever
we do for a dollar, though we wish instead
we'd done something else and may still, we never
see except with that sweet sight
that makes a tough boy shake his head.
Though taking his yearbook with him to bed
alone in the house some summer night
he'll search that stranger's face forever.

A Religious Illusion

The school bus driver had gotten down
to take his hand, and thus he was led
to his mommy at the curb. I guessed his frown
meant a tummy ache or an aching head.

And though the soul, I knew quite well,
is fanciful, abstract, unreal,
when I glanced backward out of Hell,
hers perched behind the steering wheel.

To a Graduate

What advice can I give?
I've never learned the way to live,
while the world still performs for you.
It's May and all your days dawn blue.
At noon you stretch to Heaven in
the slender sunbeam of your skin.

When I was young I was scared
and hid myself behind a beard.
I kissed no girls and wasn't kissed.
Those years have lifted like a mist
to leave me standing in the clear
with my wife and daughter near.

Clever heads will tell you how.
But was I dreaming then or now?
Dreams hand us on to other dreams
all our lives, or so it seems.
When I awake, I pray I'll keep
my silence – children need their sleep.

The Nature Lover

As a boy he half-believed
there were Indians in the trunks of trees.
Back in Indian days, his History book said,
these woods were thick with them.
Well, a whole whooping race
couldn't just vanish. He found them in woods –
they'd never left. He thought it through:

they'd been put in the trees, one to a trunk,
when the settlers were done knowing them,
and they'd just stayed put, through snows
and world wars and the coming of cars.
He was comforted sometimes walking alone
to know they were there and always watching –
wild but kindly to boys and their beagles.

And yet when they said, "That is your father
lying in that glossy box,"
he doubted it – he wasn't a man
to lie down at noon. So the son put on
his father's coat and cocked his head
the way he had, and he took him in,
to wait out winter, and all the winters.

The Moon and Me

Filling my windshield suddenly,
as round as a baby's naked bottom
yet yellow as a leaf in autumn,
the moon this morning followed me

down snowy roads as I wended
my way to work – where I made bold
to tell someone. And when I'd told,
or since I'd told, our romance ended.

When I was young, I'd try to think
a pretty girl had glanced my way.
She may have, too. I couldn't say.
But where I should have dared a wink,

I'd knit my busy brow and frown,
daring her to look again.
Those girls were wed to other men
whose suns came up, whose moons went down.

On a Daughter Gone Abroad

Peeking in her room I see
she really has gotten free,
and all her selves, remembered ones,
fill my mind like scorpions.

I should have showed her tears when I
stood at that gate and waved goodbye.
Though there were reasons not to cry
and thinking of them kept me dry.

It's just that breathing this dead air
reminds me someone once fussed here
before that mirror making straight
what God made kinky out of hate,

and that the floor that loved her junk
is bare beneath a desk and bunk.
Still if you find such pining thick,
you're right. And love's a dirty trick.

A Brief Freedom in Youth

As a boy I gazed
at slopes the late light glazed
with its purple sigh,
Everything must die.

But one time in a swoon
I climbed up to the moon
behind a bobbing braid
and barely felt afraid.

When we reached the peak
she kissed me on the cheek
inside our cozy tent
and whispered that she meant

to "take some time to think."
And I went out to blink
at lofty lights that said,
It's better being dead.

Yet driving back all day
I badgered her to stay
to see the late light glaze
the rock-face of her gaze.

Comrades

You are always advancing
while I am in constant retreat.
It's only in the barracks
that we two comrades meet.
Sugared with your triumphs,
your dreams should all be sweet.
Instead, your sleep seems frenzied
by terror or defeat.
It seems as you inspire me
to answer reveille,
you must have someone gutless
beside you while you flee.

Two on Marriage

I. The Long-Married

Although they sometimes look like longtime chums
who've vowed to be a team whatever comes,
they're lovers so far down the road they seem
one traveler against the sunset's gleam.

II. The Park

Nothing makes me feel as alone
as crossing paths with someone on her phone.

Why is it she can't see that she and I
are bride and groom beneath this sheet of sky?

Stuck in Snow

"You're spinning your wheels," I hear her nearly bray
across the frozen lawn. But we both know
I'd burn the engine out then walk away
before I'd call some jockey for a tow.

She shivers in her robe to make me see
that all I've done is prove my cussedness.
But I don't like those arms she folds at me
and her shivering only makes me like them less.

What riles me is she thinks I still have hope –
the way a fool who thinks he's innocent
even when he's hanging from a rope
still kicks against the way his verdict went.

I'll sit here till I hear the front door close.
A man must fight the devil that he knows.

Nieces on the Beach

A thousand years ago or so
they wheeled down the beach
in a glittering of cartwheels.
I didn't think they could possibly reach
the hunched toes of boulders at the end.
Since then, one has teetered into
an early marriage, while the younger
is still wheeling free as a spare tire
that will go into a lazy spin and
fall on its face in a dead clap.
Pierced by their parents' divorce,
pierced by his drug use, pierced by her
platinum resolve to get on with her life.
Plus all the usual confusion of youth.
We fly all day to see them at Christmas,
hugs and grins, but nothing
so perfect as that sparking fire-wheel
of arms and legs and sunburst
of flung hair. One was as lank
as a thoroughbred, the younger thick
and springy as a pony. They did reach
the end of the beach, and the calendar flipped
to a new year, and kept on flipping
in time with the rush of the shuttling tide.
Then this Christmas quit with a wintry scene
of snow tinted blue by the shade
of woods, and a snowy path somewhere.

Why She Went

I remember staring in a haze
at what she'd left me in a vase –
wildflowers, now dead days
and only one still at its height.
Until one day in rain-dimmed light
I saw their colors, though no longer bright,
were more intense, as if to show
the life another man would know
with her because I'd made her go –
the darkest gold, the deepest blue.
Shaving today, I smiled into
a cratered face that said, *You knew
way back when you held love at bay
you'd flourish in your own way
like wildflowers in their dark array.*

Schooled

"Well, on that bridge he watched the river run
through stony London sleeping in the sun.
He glideth at his own sweet will,
he wrote, as though the Thames had time to kill,
or was a young lad running off to sea,
reminding Wordsworth he was young and free."
"Did you always want to teach?" a tall girl sighs,
and all the wind that puffed my sails dies.

"I *never* did. I'm not sure why I'm here.
When you start out, you do things on a dare –
to test your strength, and then to pay the rent,
as you guys go to school because you're sent.
Though did you ever wonder how it is
the earth and moon come close and never kiss,
but praise the sun while trading doubtful looks?
That's why we're here . . . Page 18 in your books."

Why Old Men Should Be Sad

Sometimes now I think
of my mother at the sink,
tapping at the pane
if it began to rain –
or sometimes just to wave
as she can't from her grave.

Though nothing is destroyed
to vanish in the void,
soon my crumbs will leach
down runnels beyond reach
where they'll forget their name
and mine were once the same.

ABOUT THE AUTHOR

Don Barkin has published poems in *Poetry, The Virginia Quarterly Review, Prairie Schooner, Poetry Northwest,* the *North American Review, Harvard Magazine, The Louisville Review, Commonweal,* and other journals. A full-length collection of his poems, *That Dark Lake,* published by Antrim House in 2009, was a finalist for the Connecticut Center for the Book's poetry award. His two chapbooks, *The Caretakers* and *The Persistent,* have been published by Finishing Line Press, and he has twice been awarded artist grants by the State of Connecticut. A former newspaper reporter, he was educated at Harvard and Cambridge Universities. He has taught writing at Yale, Wesleyan, and Connecticut College, and now teaches school near New Haven, Connecticut, where he lives with his wife, Maggie, and his daughter, Eve.

This book is set in Garamond Premier Pro, which had its genesis in 1988 when type-designer Robert Slimbach visited the Plantin-Moretus Museum in Antwerp, Belgium, to study its collection of Claude Garamond's metal punches and typefaces. During the mid-fifteen hundreds, Garamond—a Parisian punch-cutter—produced a refined array of printing types that combined an unprecedented degree of balance and elegance, for centuries standing as the pinnacle of beauty and practicality in type-founding. Slimbach has created an entirely new interpretation based on Garamond's designs and on compatible italics cut by Robert Granjon, Garamond's contemporary.

To order additional copies of this book
or other Antrim House titles, contact the publisher at

Antrim House
21 Goodrich Rd., Simsbury, CT 06070
860.217.0023, AntrimHouse@comcast.net
or the house website (www.AntrimHouseBooks.com).

•

On the house website
in addition to information on books
you will find sample poems, upcoming events,
and a "seminar room" featuring supplemental biography,
notes, images, poems, reviews, and
writing suggestions.

www.ingramcontent.com/pod-product-compliance
Lightning Source LLC
Chambersburg PA
CBHW021447080526
44588CB00009B/731